I0789420

FEMALE POWER DRIVE
Liberal Feminist Tyranny and Scapegoats

by Karen Kellock Ph.D.

Manual for
Superior Men

A complete theory based on Einstein physics,
Political Psychology, Systems Theory
and Archetypal Psychiatry.

FORMULA

All success attraction
All disease obstruction
All recovery elimination

You must fast on all three

OBSTRUCTIONS:

People
Habit
Food

FEMALE POWER DRIVE

Hold your head up high: be ready for jealous slights. For sweet little ladies winning thru subtle spiritual power are gone, replaced by big harridans. Talking to them you feel ripped apart. They start out sweet then the evil starts.   They get restless when things are harmonious and go on the attack: every man knows this.   There's no guards on their mind: outa nowhere they pick fights and here we go again, cycles of fright.

FEMALE POWER DRIVE

Liberal Feminist Tyranny and Scapegoats

FEMALE POWER DRIVE

Liberal Feminist Tyranny and Scapegoats

FEMALE POWER DRIVE
Liberal Feminist Tyranny and Scapegoats

FEMINIST FALLOUT

All dad ever said was "hold your head up high" and I think he meant be ready for jealous slights.

The female power drive came at me like a bat outa hell. I shudder to think how she crushed my Self.

Male anger is frightening but there's something about the deep dark cavern of her wrath see.

Once she has you in sight she gets on the horn and engages everyone to fight: female fright.

My frenemy used Al-Anon as a forum to gossip about me out of "concern" and this is the girls.

The sweet little ladies winning thru subtle spiritual power are gone, replaced by big harridans.

You can't talk to any of em without feeling ripped apart. They start out sweet then the evil starts.

You handle people problems by avoiding em. Navigate your ship skillfully avoiding fake friends.

SHE DEGRADES YOUR IDENTITY

Without knowledge I impart here you may feel degraded, obsolete, inferior after being with her.

If mama's not happy ain't nobody happy in the house and this is something they all know first.

FEMALE POWER DRIVE

The more wrong she is the more contentious and imperious and thus starts the system mess.

She's sticky like fly paper. Once you're in her craw she never lets up till you're scorned in the gutter.

Most women are liberal, that's a fact. This creates an environment of vacuity, hostility and tyranny.

You say ONE word indicating you're out of the accepted matrix and they attack you as treacherous.

They get restless when things are too harmonious and go on the attack: every man knows this.

There's no guards on her mind. Outa nowhere she picks fights and here we go again, cycles of fright.

FEMALE ATTACK ON NOVELTY

Some women are very gregarious with female culture but the odd nerds are attacked for sure.

They fight almost exclusively thru backstabbing gossip so controlling it becomes a bargaining chip.

When people hear these things they tuck em away and there they stay--gossip is dangerous ok.

The problem is backstabbers are idiots, controlled by social hypnotists and thus you've had it.

When they're not looking in all the drawers for valuables they're instigating riots/creating troubles.

What has happened to people? They give you a welcome dinner then mercilessly insult you.

The housekeeper wanted to talk to me after her work then proceeded to stealthily soul murder.

FEMALE POWER DRIVE

Either work thru a foreman, a computer or avoid any help altogether. Or meet on tasks, particular.

For that Dunning-Kruger is in effect and when a Spirit of Familiarity comes over it becomes a hex.

Cease seeing them as people and see em as demons attracted to weakness and get free now.

After talking to her I felt whipped/chastised for days. There's something so vicious in her ways.

What has happened to people? They give you a welcome dinner then insult you as a sinner.

SUBTLE SLIGHTS

It's so subtle too. Like bats in the night the put downs swing past and just for peace we deny it all.

The sickening thing is its couched in maudlin, syrupy virtue signaling which nauseates clear minds.

Just stay close to a trusted inner circle and by the way they're all on probation too you know.

A feminist type may flake out suddenly. Like all liberals she's lured by fantasy then cuts back see.

A combo of fantasy and irritability creates relationships of high variability and it's too much for me.

After one encounter with a female ragaholic I shudder to think about it and may never get over it.

DUNNING-KRUGER EFFECT

Yours is a Triumph of Ideas. It's taken half a century but you are finally there, whole and poised.

FEMALE POWER DRIVE

What I went thru with the Dunning-Kruger Effect of the dumb thinking they're smart was a hex.

I was a stranger in a strange land, an alien. They were bigger than me/all the women hated me.

We're winning everywhere. It's a season of winning as I see my enemies disperse, gone, vapor.

The hedge is up, we're winning and foes are toast. It runs like a Swiss watch: joy in the household.

Everyone has illusions of their self but this girl was so touchy she went to war like to a bell.

After the last attack you stop calling out going inward to a world of fantasy, joy and thought.

Your life's an open book in a liberal town or clan. It's all based on gossip and infights among them.

It's like they sock you in the face through the computer then for days and weeks you suffer.

Relax for there were never any true perceptions just magnetisms of the moment, all gone.

PERCEPTION IS RELATIONAL

Perception was you vis-a-vis them: the system. Memory changes with self-esteem son.

The Hero's Path was rocky and terrifying. I couldn't trust anyone, all rose up against me see.

But everything has a middle and an end, I can promise you that my friend. You'll end in heaven.

But this won't last forever, the terrible pain of being misunderstood and judged for whatever.

FEMALE POWER DRIVE

It's when you're still too immature to handle it but different enough to bring a LOT of rebuff.

I had a chip on my shoulder a mile wide. Who wouldn't, being misjudged constantly by the snide?

Suddenly I saw they were all like that so I stopped getting hung up on any one/just took naps.

Just expect em to abuse you cuz they will. This isn't the fifties, we live in a deceptive human jungle.

GOD WORKS THRU INDIVIDUALS

God works thru individuals, only this is genius--it's blocked when freedom is lost/conformists.

Is it real music or screeches from hell--can you even tell at this stage of seared conscience/smell?

It was a Pyrrhic Victory: She won the argument but I never wanna see the vicious human again.

He actually erases the past. I must tell y'all of this wonderful supernatural gift and blast.

I love solitude of a cabin in the wilderness but hate it when people come by making a mess.

My nice alcoholic husband became Putinian: he didn't just wanna injure me but go for a killin'

When I told him I was a "vessel" that didn't go in the med school and then I lost my grants too.

It's the Erasure of the Past which is the good news of the gospel. Everyone wants to start over.

An older woman is just into her home and that's a big part of the attraction, old fashioned.

FEMALE POWER DRIVE

All that crap provided the fodder and the fire to write these books on social psych archetypes.

R AND R BETWEEN ATTACKS

I celebrate writer's block cuz it gives me a break from this, in preparation for the next blitz.

She was sticking you a little, poking the bear, flushing you out. That's how they work it student.

A hostile reaction was due to your differences not your badness, get that straight your highness.

I want one person who loves and understands me to tell me how to live well not a bunch of people.

A queen knows enough to guard her heart but a maid doesn't know that and is totally torn apart.

A queen won't accept lowdown positions of passersby, she's shut in to home, to others bye bye.

She was such a strong ass bitch the trauma of my older sisters came back to me then an itch.

I admire anyone who's competent and diligent, not wanting fame/fortune just for being born.

If you compress a spring it will snap back hard. That's what happened to me thru those years.

A razor sharp tongue/apt words to put down. Loud screeches from hell: her son's a musician.

I did not define you, you defined yourself by your words but you can't see that yet: need to learn.

The bible says not to markup your bodies like the heathen do so I guess you're a hick Sue.

FEMALE POWER DRIVE

PEOPLE CAN GET LIKE HITLER

People can get like Hitler: better believe her. Anyone can if they have the upper hand sir.

Never take her back to prove she's wrong. The rift's still in your craw, you wanna win that's all.

Ellen brought a generation of teen age girls into lesbianism, an example of social hypnotism.

Feminism isn't about voting/equal pay but a Victim Mentality Disorder and the culprits are men, ok?

Men are being fired and replaced by women on accusation alone. The end is here, Lord come.

When accusation becomes conviction of course women will use that in pursuit of their occupations.

You win by avoiding them. I've laid out signs indicating you're better off alone not these "friends".

For God will always bring one good friend who may be hidden due to your bad associations.

SHE'S ALWAYS VICTIM/HE'S ALWAYS CULPRIT

Women have established themselves as perpetual victims who always need to be compensated by men.

Identity politics: You are worthy or unworthy not by your behavior but by your identity--ridiculous.

You have no power to change your designation of victim or culprit, you're forever guilty/a mean prick.

Big corporations and everyone promoting by gender: It's happening all over and it's inefficient/unfair.

FEMALE POWER DRIVE

Feminism has become so powerful a man accused of rape has to prove his innocence not his guilt, ok?

Men are so intimidated cowering before women it's pathetic and sad and we want men back.

All men wear a body cam or bring back the presumption of innocence! For they've wiped it out fast.

The feminist world acts like accusations are reality. They ride with it, fire the best and have no empathy.

All my life I felt accused by women. I had to be so careful so as to not trigger that female demon.

RUINED BY ACCUSATION ALONE

Accusation to Ruin: They sought to ruin me and succeeded greatly all due to my naiveté.

Anything novel or different triggered angry persecution of one's unique differences: by liberals/feminists.

There's always ulterior motives and if accusation alone works, hey! You think they don't use it?

The Dominance and Effects of Ideological Feminism is pivotal to the end of our world and happiness.

The craziest stuff you ever heard/could conceive comes out of universities by ideological feminists.

I adapted to mom by introjection--swallowing whole--and became her when drunk or mad like a role.

MOM WAS THE FIRST FEMINIST I MET

She was the first feminist in my life, an outrageously strong figure, then my two older sisters.

FEMALE POWER DRIVE

They were mostly women but men were docile and weakened tho' grateful to be hooked in thru them.

Women would get ANGRY at my differences so I chose isolation very early, the only way to be happy.

Think of the effects on personality by squelching or stretching self to fit her preconceived notions.

Women are dominant and men are nice--I saw that at an early age before pedophiles and road rage.

You just must give up on the female community and be in a category all by yourself--no pegging a magic elf.

I would so much rather have a chosen man over me rather than society, neighbors, cops or agencies.

He protects me so I can expand within the home. It is freedom, doing my own thing, paradise come.

Instead of wearing your heart on your sleeve/airing your dirty laundry, say "no man knows my history."

NARCISSIST MOMS FEED ON YOUR PAIN

A narcissist mother will get high off your pain. She'll ground you right before a great date.

It's her lack of empathy which is most disturbing. A narcissistic mom drives her kids crazy.

It wasn't in your head when you saw that little smirk on your mothers face when you were crying.

A narcissistic mom puts your dog to sleep without telling you, for no reason at all--did that start your fall?

They weren't thinking of you--they were dismissive and negligent and now you only expect that.

FEMALE POWER DRIVE

With attentive and loving parents no one decides to accept a dismissive, apathetic relationship.

With a loving background a poor relationship is an instant turnoff but not to the offspring of narcissists.

Comparing you to other kids: basically saying they got the short end of the stick by having such a twit.

GOLDEN CHILD AND BLACK SHEEP

The narcissist mom splits between her Golden Child and the Black Sheep and these become scripts.

The Black Sheep is made to know they don't matter and are inadequate compared to the Golden script.

The Black Sheep role is so obdurate/hard to change only superhuman strength transcends it, to fame.

The Golden Child relies on his imputed image and ends flat on his face as everything reverses late.

She loves the IMAGE the Golden Child presents--not real love--but it's the Black Sheep she berates.

The Black Sheep is actually the narcissist's extension--a VERY dark image-- and I was that odd woman.

Mom was always crying over the Golden Child but when it came to me it was "we had one too many".

I was the problem child. That was my identity which became my script on how to act--WILD.

MOM LIVES FOR DRAMA

They live for drama. They live for high, explosive emotional reactions so watch your pets son.

FEMALE POWER DRIVE

The narc can't feel so must make you feel to vicariously live thru it. It's so sad you can't get over it.

The problem is the group treats you as bad as mom does and won't allow your growth beyond it.

You think they're getting in your head to help you but it's to rile you up, get you upset, make you nuts.

You must question every single motive. When you converse does it end in tears or are you motivated?

He's so disordered he actually prefers self-destructive attacks to getting along in peace/no static.

When they needed a "sit down" it's cuz they're running low on drama and supply--that was family.

People get bored and restless so decide to stir things up: get emotional reaction for supply/fill thy cup.

It comes as quite a shock to realize these people have deliberately been hindering you but it's true.

Not only was love withheld, as you got older they played emotional games with you for their own supply.

TRIGGERING FEAR WITHOUT EMPATHY

It's bad being a child of a narcissist as they're compelled to trigger fear and rage yet have no empathy.

A smart child asks questions and that's seen as a challenge to authority, a punishable anomaly.

A narcissistic injury is when one sees thru his fake persona and he can't handle the trauma.

Tell him what he is and you'll hear a torrent of cuss words seemingly out of character but not that rare.

FEMALE POWER DRIVE

As the two sisters got her captive they tortured her emotionally for years, that was the setup.

When she went bankrupt you really saw the setup. They had a field day: "you're poor so shut up."

Dear Lord it was so demeaning to be around these meanies--my own sisters the two feminazis.

Why be so cruel in putting one down? Because it's an IDENTITY struggle: I'm good/you're a clown.

It's a gestalt: we see ourselves against the ground of the other--it defines us so we keep it together.

Why did they erupt in calumnious slander and gossip? Cuz that's their nature, you have to see it.

CINDERELLA SYNDROME

The Cinderella Syndrome was so entrenched they literally had to die out for little sister to have clout.

Everyone listened to the "elders"--they're the majority and older and they all want to hate the younger.

You have to see that these liberals in your family are democrats--evil, you're the victim of rats.

You may be the only conservative in your family save ancestors who have passed. It's very sad.

Why is the Cinderella Syndrome so inveterate? Because it's. WOMEN and they never give up a grudge.

When women warp from their true destiny they are the worst of all honey and I mean. TREACHERY.

I love privacy, I've always been that way. So please don't come and also tell your friends to stay away.

FEMALE POWER DRIVE

I'm not at all independent. I own two cars but don't even drive and I need protection to fully thrive.

CHRISTIANITY IS EXCLUSIVE

Christianity is exclusive not inclusive. It's about drawing lines because you can't unify with evil see.

When you hear "unity" go the other way. Good can never unify with evil--that's only new age falsity.

I'm gonna laugh when you eat your words. When you face it was FRAUD putting your guy first.

God of mine: operates outside of time but He always delivers our needed blessings just in time.

There's a phase of necessary isolation before success so don't see this period as a death sentence.

Thinking about past abusers constantly is like crying over them again--use self-control or you'll sin.

ELECTION FRAUD

So now we're stuck in "election denialism"? There's always a new jargon to what they're pushin

Go ahead Joe, steal the election--see instant retribution for what we've been thru since the last one.

Trump's phenomenal campaigning proves the fallacy of ageism cuz we're dynamos until our last breath baby.

Will they still love Biden when he transfers their country to the globalist hellscape on the horizon?

World government via economic collapse, viral plagues released and the 3rd world overtaking the first

FEMALE POWER DRIVE

It's the idea our own votes as citizens can be cancelled out by illegal votes, that's the point man.

95% of the media is anti-Trump. That's nearly impossible to overcome by a candidate but we didn't give up.

This was a fraudulent election which like all of em is evinced in ridiculous and improbable spikes.

100,000 ballots all for Biden. The odds of that are so preposterously low it's false on prima facie alone.

I haven't turned on Fox. On getting hurt like that again I can't take a chance.

AOC: BAD BUSINESS

AOC has a million dollar slush fund after condemning dark money and she even wants to take our guns.

One sign of the Jezebel Spirit: The minute she gets into power she completely and brutally takes over.

Is it better to have aggressively ignorant but attractive faces at the head of your party than someone smart?

AOC is just another communist fake on the take.

AOC is approaching in her own mind Goddess Status. It's an I-am-God phase of the new age asses.

It's dangerous and yes she is taking over--not cuz she's so great but cuz they're so dumb: God, come!

ELIMINATION OF ALL WHITE MEN

The elimination of the white man, the new social pariah, has become an inherent moral good in the culture.

I am conservative, sisters were liberals. Liberals don't change, they become more full of themselves.

FEMALE POWER DRIVE

Is it better to have aggressively ignorant but attractive faces at the head of your party than someone smart?

You have no idea how scary this all is--Cortez. The fact others love her could mean America's END.

It's the idea you don't have to check a good sounding idea against what actually happens. Thomas Sowell

One sign of the Jezebel Spirit: The minute she gets into power she completely and brutally takes over.

Get this straight: We're not scared of Cortez we're scared of her influence over dumbed minds.

AOC's a virtue signaling tyrant who doesn't know a thing. Her talks are boring and discrepant, rinky-dink.

Donald Trump speaks logic/common sense, AOC speaks rot/gibberish--they couldn't be more different.

Don't dare compare that idiot AOC with the King! The Great White Hope makes sense/our heart sing.

EVERY GOOD REASON TO HATE HER

AOC: We have every reason to hate her. It's just common sense to fear an evil charismatic influencer.

Is Congresswoman Cortez against abortion, late term? NO--she's says nothing about this curse.

I hate calling her AOC--a sign of familiarity--cuz this woman is horrible in the things she's suggesting.

No comparisons between AOC and Trump--Donald speaks logic and common sense/she speaks crud.

AOC is embarrassingly ignorant in her $3000 pantsuits talkin' about poor folks then destroying their jobs.

FEMALE POWER DRIVE

AOC proves Millennials are into looks-only, pure superficiality. To the dumbed down she's a real smarty.

The stuff AOC advocates is horrible and deadly but she says it sweetly in her niceties to the peanut gallery.

How could you love horrible harridan tyrant AOC--who wants to trash our prosperity/control everything?

All common sense, logic, history, precedent or law be damned--AOC who looks good leads the land!

Our president's not afraid of AOC but her evil INFLUENCE. Lucifer looks good but the world's worst menace.

It's AOC's brazen narcissism--dancin' for the cameras but not applaudin' for America's prosperity/protection.

AOC's a narcissistic attention- whore and it's immature. Get some respect for those who know more.

PUPPET CONGRESSWOMAN: BUSINESS IS BAD

Progressives like Cortez trained to think business is bad--they'll even applaud when unemployed are sad.

The VERY scary thing is ACO's influence--a measure of the vastness of her dumbed-down fan base.

It's not that people want to earn what they get but socialism has never worked it's just the elite it benefits.

Socialists always promise to benefit the middle class who then starves as food is used as a weapon.

All dictators whether Stalin or Hitler delete/ban all information revealing all their many contradictions.

They are TYRANTS and the first order of business is our SPEECH cuz how else could we object to creeps?

FEMALE POWER DRIVE

I was disinvited out of a refusal to be dictated to about what I was to say or what I could not say.

HA HA The democrats wanted to harness the glory of their youngest star member: not too clever!

JEXIT: Jews are leaving the dems cuz who wants to vote for people who won't chastise your enemies?

AOC is a very scary phenomenon seeing the HYPNOTIC potential one can have like the dangerous Rasputin.

Are you against being a Nazi? Then why are you acting like one?

EFFECTS OF FEMALE POWER DRIVE ON STATE

Socialism TAKES and capitalism CREATES.

People's Revolutions are top-down hierarchy of CONTROL. Everyone's a dam bully and it's awful, I know.

It's the biggest load of naiveté to think the ruling class of USSR or China were concerned for the "workers".

It's the idea you don't have to check a good sounding idea against what actually happens. Thomas Sowell

Communism always begins with "STRUGGLE": transforming society through conflicts between groups.

Christianity, capitalism and Americana is *individualism*--a notion prohibited in a struggle towards communism.

Thinking of your self as an individual is not allowed as Marxism interfaces with the identity movement.

I wasn't sufficiently inoculated against my generation so naively let em in and was even influenced by em.

Bible speaks of evil men hypnotizing weak women in their homes. Get some class, draw a line, stay alone.

FEMALE POWER DRIVE

In a world that's insane would you rather be controversial or acceptable?

There's always strings attached and the most invisible WILL become visible--don't ever forget that!

COASTAL LIBS HATE FLYOVER STATES

Flyover: People who have loyalty, who have honor, who will back you up when attacked or in a corner.

Elitist hatred of middle America is a projection of their own evil while wishing they were real like them.

Bill Maher gave the green light for coastal utopians to abuse middle Americans, the last liberty bastions.

Only a stuck pig squeals. Hollywood's attacks on middle America are because they've lost all appeal.

Bill Maher--the coastal liberal elites--put down middle America's morals and family values as obsolete.

One definition of socialism is the collection of power into fewer and fewer hands. Michael Savage

Socialists confess a love of diversity but they insist on absolute conformity. Donald J. Trump

I won the wealthy places which are optimistic, diverse, dynamic and moving forward--the *coasts*. Hillary Clinton

Socialism spends the money that capitalism creates. No one can deny that even the Millennial ingrates.

The very idea posers like AO Cortez has a huge twitter following shows it's all inferior and I'm withdrawing.

LIBERALISM: THE DEFAULT STINK

Via marriage my family had been taken over by another culture. Since I was still enmeshed, it was torture.

FEMALE POWER DRIVE

I go crazy in liberal environments, they make me sick--it's a combo of arrogance and evil without restraint.

The things libs believe in are despicable, appalling, unbelievable, nonsensical--and you're their pal?

Your weakness was a magnet to their compulsion to take, control, use, abuse then throw you to wolves.

Joseph's brothers tried to kill him then sold him as a slave. Women are worse so how did sis behave?

I'm telling you--don't argue with em! The bible says it: no futile debates with scum! Babykillers all of them.

Once you give in at one level it all collapses: it's ALWAYS more more more. Nip it in the bud, then soar.

When you finally refuse to debate them or change their mind you get all that energy back and it's sublime.

I sense a liberal in one second. They can't hide it nor can we as they sense and hate the patriots.

Just one word or gesture shows you as liberal--it's your reactions to things, theories and other folderol.

RACES AND GENDERS ARE TOTALLY DIFFERENT

The idea there's no difference between the races is just ridiculous.

The idea there's no difference between genders is the stupidest idea in all of history's revisers.

God made us male and female. It is important for women to be feminine and men to be masculine.

Sacred masculinity: channeled aggression, stoicism, self-control, ambition, honor, fury when necessary.

FEMALE POWER DRIVE

Millennials seem scared of what I say even though it was just common sense in an earlier day, oh my...

The gender ideologues have already lost the scientific front so now take it to the legislative and other stunts.

Transgenderism is not rooted in mainstream science but emotional superstition dominates the conversation.

Hollywood was seducing me but it was so empty I didn't want it so I built my own operation as separate.

A form of narcissism embraces Hollywood culture. For who could possibly back that? Evil or the immature.

Hotness fades, wisdom grows.

Hollywood culture is divorced from reality, hateful, decadent and empty seeking to make us just as nasty.

Wherever there's most porn there's most plastic surgery as poor wives compete with teens the husband likes.

Pornography is a demon sent from hell to snag you, pull you down and destroy the family completely.

HOLLYWOOD AND BETRAYAL TRAUMA

Don't trivialize Betrayal Trauma. Someone you thought you knew is really a cad into girlie pictures too.

If money fixes things affluence blocks repentance and *that's* why heaven's blocked to those with riches.

As repeated by witch Kamela Harris, "the bourgeoise family is passe and must be eliminated: Karl Marx.

Universal Housing is where you come home from work and find people living in all your rooms with perks.

FEMALE POWER DRIVE

I don't have time for glib talk: it's like that whiny music in department stores with brainwashed college folk.

Socialism always goes against human nature which is why it ALWAYS devolves to tyranny. Donald Trump

Green New Deal is actually the litmus test for those vying for the highest office in the land. Lord, what a scam!

Socialists never come to power by telling em: "We're gonna take your stuff and you're gonna starve".

Now let me get this straight: a young and beautiful but very dumb woman takes over America's fate?

There have been no penalties for hate hoaxes, only rewards.

America is NOT a hateful country--it's the most welcoming place on earth. Reject those liars, a curse.

Societies eventually collapse under weight of their own accumulated complexity and bureaucracy.

VICTIMOLOGY: SUFFERING BETTER THAN ACHIEVING

Victimology: It is better to suffer than it is to achieve.

GLOBAL EUROPA is white people preserving and appreciating their differences which are best of all.

Liberalism: deranged frothing at the mouth hysteria combined with embracing Islam which hates America.

The left has embraced Islamism the most intolerant belief system on earth: intimidation and violence.

What about what they do to dogs, let alone women? It's false religion.

They're silencing voices they don't like/amplifying voices they do like and we're fighting for our life.

FEMALE POWER DRIVE

Bill Maher doesn't understand America where family, faith and freedom are at the center of their lives.

They hate him tho' Trump rescued the economy, stood up to our enemies, revived national pride and jobs.

Capitalism has flaws but socialism has no benefits. Lee Cooperman

Never let democrats forget they're the part of Jim Crow, segregation, slavery and the KKK. NEVER, ok?

Rebuilt military, cut taxes, destroyed ISIS/Iran deal, Rocketman, deregulation, Kavanaugh on bench.

Democracy fails because they vote in socialism. We're not a democracy we elect reps and leave it to em.

Democrats/Pelosi: Going nowhere, hopelessly divided and chasing down the rabbit hole of socialism.

MEANINGLESS MEASURES AGAINST "HATE"

House passes broad measure against "hate" but that's just a way to catch conservatives: bad fate.

Get this thru your head: virtue signaling is not religion or Christianity--it's just you getting approval you see.

It's the moral self-righteousness of liberals (just know they're superior) while being so immoral.

You say something and they're gone. These are friends with narrow threshhold limits: reject, new song.

You say something and she's gone, then comes back only to do it again when you said something, oh man!

SCAPEGOATISM

One solitary Christian in a family of female liberals. Fighting this resistance was a terrible hell.

FEMALE POWER DRIVE

The people claiming to love me spoke behind my back horribly. These were my own sisters, unbelievably.

They just don't like you, period. Stop trying to change their mind, get on with it. You're too much, wizard!

Decades after scapegoat leaves family system she discovers it was *liberalism* driving it all down!

Difference between liberals vs. conservatives explained it all--a relief to know why growth was stalled.

It was so horrible being treated like a thing. To be made decisions for no matter what I wanted, so revealing...

My mother—the bad mother element--was also feminist but made insane with continuous drunkenness.

I didn't feel loved, valued or understood. As a sensitive child with unmet love needs I was dense as wood.

How to adapt to beta/absent dads and feminist drunk mothers? De-program or continue getting dumber.

The scapegoat is aware and hypersensitive to the truth of what's going on-- the pseudo-mutual CON.

Now clear you'll naturally attract the right niche, group, following, fanbase, satellites, brethren, whatever.

SCAPEGOAT BACKGROUND

Scapegoat: a constant undercurrent of sibling rivalry, competition, and fighting for parental attention.

The mother fears the black sheep who's the only one with enough courage to confront the creeps.

In narcissistic families there's an emotional pain that's kept hidden.

FEMALE POWER DRIVE

Scapegoat feels he has no rights in the family, no right to speak, just a thing but not in the room, a creep.

Scapegoat is told **NOT TO FEEL** his very normal feelings which are deep, primal, lonely, frightening, sickening.

After going thru all the people problems of feminists in control I built so much good overcoming muscle!

Any discussion with a liberal feminist brought frustration, resentment and a sense of being unfree.

Women think with their heart anyway, but when the conscience is seared it's just phony virtue signaling.

And the liberal feminist Millennials are many times worse. They're course, crass and debauched of course.

The duchess was complicated: cold, mean-spirited, a bully and sadistic.

Uncompleted mourning: After sister separation I gravitated to the same type of liberal female irritation.

FEMINIST FEMALES ARE NOT FRIENDS

Feminist females can **NOT** be your friends. The things they believe in are immoral so keep distance!

The sister-wives culture is like crabs in a barrel: they hold each other down-- drop em all to be renowned.

Think of how men have taken on personalities of their liberal feminist mothers just cuz dad wasn't there!

Since liberal feminist women are crazy and the kids reflect em, no wonder we're in deep trouble/no kiddin'.

Compare the slim little ladies so charming of the fifties and compare with these foulmouthed tattooed slutties!

FEMALE POWER DRIVE

Liberal mothers encouraged girls to love Hillary and hate Trump--just another example of going wrong.

My white protestant (Calvinist) Americana family was taken over by a Hindu in 1964 as they all drank beer.

My Christian mother and I protested to the sudden incursion of another culture who said they were better.

She can't set the agenda, she must tow the line. Most adapt but some cannot--that was me always crying.

As the family scapegoat (cuza how I thought) I felt surrounded by strangers, excruciating pain in gut.

The feeling of dis-unity and rejection was so great an eating disorder took over, a progression of bad fate.

EXILE FROM SCAPEGOAT SYSTEMS

The more enmeshed in the family system the more deep the hurt with rejection but I found God/salvation.

I exiled to the desert wilderness for 27 years and overcame fear: of the dark, of loneliness, of family not near.

My sisters acted like I didn't exist. They only gossiped and laid bad seeds about me the sickest.

Family scapegoat suffers *ontologically fatal insight* that life, world, people were not what they thought.

What does a Hindu and Christians have in common? Nothing so they just drank beer acting real lovin'.

I couldn't wait to get away but still weak, attracted the same. A gang of boys invaded me: more pain.

What did I learn from all this? INVASION the problem, need fences, walls, boundaries, being ALONE!

FEMALE POWER DRIVE

It hurts being objectified: ageism is the worst. It's as bad as racism as they smell money after hearse.

Lacking healthy boundaries after the sick family system I had no defenses later and got enmeshed again.

Enmeshed, eclipsed by another, I would lose my happy reality of creativity. Independence, please!

Staying free and independent (mentally, creatively) became paramount. My cozy little office, that's all.

As a psychologist I see the SYSTEM as the whole thing. We adapted to them and that made us crazy.

WE'RE NOT ALL ONE: STOP INVADING ME

We're not ALL ONE and all religions are NOT THE SAME so to DIVIDE was why the savior Christ came.

The worst was when they came without calling. The invasion of privacy was painful and appalling.

Being invaded in my privacy space hurt physically. It messed me up for hours, really--was I just crazy?

Solitude and privacy is an inalienable right in the constitution but the liberals call it "social anxiety disorder".

Bible speaks of evil men hypnotizing weak women in their homes. Get some class, draw a line, stay alone.

Don't chastise yourself for letting evil men in--you were weaker then, you even needed their approval woman!

You were so needy you craved him coming over. It's only now you see the devastation every hour.

I know you're angry--who wouldn't be? He's coming over just for sex when you're about love/monogamy.

FEMALE POWER DRIVE

Nothing's worse than being dominated in your own home by a man you let in when you preferred to be alone.

You wanted to be alone, he pressured you to let him in, you did and became mentally ill = his rejection.

It is the most abundant and profitable past-time: looking out the window musing--it's a gold mine.

They call her a heretic but Joyce Meyers resurrected my goals and gave me joyous hope, what a gal.

Through a weak alcoholic husband the devil comes right through to the wife esp. if she's God's woman.

Why ever leave home? All my things are there. It's never anything better on the outside than it is in here!

GETTING YOU TO LEAVE HOME

They can't stand I'm happy in here. They want me out there--on their turf--knowing for me it's bad fare.

There's nothing I can do with them I don't enjoy more by myself. No one's as good as the magic elf.

Since the postwar new age SOCIAL is the whole thing. There's a conspiracy against privacy and it stinks.

If you'd rather be alone than be bored with them it may bring violence since social's the whole thing.

Social expectations are so engrained even police dared to ask me: "Why DON'T you want them here?"

Church ladies acted so put upon, so insulted, that I preferred to stay home--now a woman's place is chattin'

Devil knows how sacred the home is but since it's been degraded he lures us out to waste time all day.

FEMALE POWER DRIVE

Due to the conspiracy against privacy you must put your foot down--just say "NO" and turn/no more talk.

They'd rather stay home but too wimpy to insist so they make sure YOU go out to be bored and pissed.

Prescription for Misfits: Stop all social expectations immediately.   Retire into joy: unplanned days being free.

They want you to leave home because they're such empty boring people they need you to proffer em up.

If they had anything going they'd wanna stay home themselves--an exciting inner journey enriched.

THE OUTER IS COMPLETELY EMPTY

The empty are outer--they need other things! The abundant are inner: it's the rich life of the soul they seek.

If a cat hisses at a dog I put her in her room. She's obviously better with privacy and feels much better too.

Along with desire for solitude is cerebrotonia: fear of disorder. This goes along with disgust with others.

We're supposed to work not chat. WORK is part of the Christian tradition but chattering's as bad as fat.

The more totally ignored you are now the more a SPLASH you'll be later--it works that way brother.

It's hard to believe no one's imposing on me. Even with a wall/locked gate I'm so used to being unfree.

The church ladies bugged me half to death to leave my comfy sanctuary to go to their potlucks so boring.

By walking away/going no-contact with narcissistic abusers your voice is finally heard loud and clear.

FEMALE POWER DRIVE

I will not take your abuse any longer. I have had enough, no more. I'm going to where I'm loved as seer.

Dear scapegoat: Only thru your silence can they hear all the words you tried to speak but was bashed.

Abuse: Being blamed for everything going wrong in the dysfunctional family-- you're a scapegoat, truly.

The scapegoat walks away to the best life he's ever known, free of abuse-- boundaries, respect, so cool!

The new family (good system) is CHOSEN based on respect as the first priority and I'm loving them.

EXILED TO A WILDERNESS CABIN

Kicked out to the wilderness in a cabin and bicycle--nearly zero--but that opened me to God my Hero.

What happens to the abusers the scapegoat leaves behind--to the dynamics of the system so blind?

What happens when the appointed family Trash Can walks away? Ha ha now we really see a sick display.

There's a huge gaping hole left creating disturbance in all family members, mass destruction remembers.

Everything is destroyed when the truth comes out: Garbage thrown back with appointed Trash Can gone.

They huddle together in "love" but begin to distance as scapegoat tendency spreads out evenly.

They unite in their hatred of scapegoat, bringing them closer together. I recall being so sequestered.

They side against him constantly and will NOT listen to reason. He's a stranger in a strange land of treason.

FEMALE POWER DRIVE

I knew how much gossiping and trash-talking was taking place. I could feel the grapevine of my disgrace.

When I went to a new town they laid evil seeds against me wanting them to hate me too--God, can this be?

Once scapegoat is gone narcissistic family self-destructs--remembering how they him like a mutt!

RX FOR THE APPOINTED TRASH CAN

Self-gentleness is key. The more leisure breaks I take the better, a resuscitation of genius all for free.

They told me I was bad for being white while justifying the most horrible things in a sickening blight.

They made me feel guilty at age 16 for driving a Mustang. "White privilege" way back then, now cresting.

But then they adorned their POCs with everything--mansions, cars, ivy league educations--while rejecting me.

Severe trust issues and strained relationships in the remaining family members of the scapegoat system.

Though family members can't admit to being thugs deep down it's impossible to sweep it under the rug.

The deafening silence of the scapegoat's absence is a loud siren scream from deep inside the same kin.

It's way too intense not to make the narcissistic family face this fact every single day--karma's a bitch, ok?

They try to numb the pain of the scapegoat's absence but always reminded he's no longer there as dunce.

The other members are sick, yes--but not braindead enough not to be affected by the scapegoat's absence.

FEMALE POWER DRIVE

You treated me like I didn't exist then my whole life was amiss 'till I found God and my one true Existence.

Since you spouted liberal narrative and the whole culture did too/plus the schools only you were "true".

Since I wanted to be feminine, create a home and other feminine things you called me mad and weak.

To repeat, they are **NOT** braindead enough not to be **SEVERELY** affected by the absence of the scapegoat.

The absence of the exiled scapegoat they hated so much changes them and their world = out-to-lunch.

The scapegoat has walked away and everyone is shocked by the deafening sounds of their footsteps.

RX IS NO-CONTACT WHATSOEVER

I was not allowed to feel or speak my truth, but by walking away **NO-CONTACT** my voice spoke to my roots.

When you need a target for your own projections and the target is gone it mis-shoots and goes wrong.

It was **ALWAYS** two-against-one. My slogan was "triangulation is strangulation" as I prayed to God.

Heard there was nothing worse than a Kellock female in control. When they got in power, watch out fools.

Women are tyrants--that's why a generation is mentally ill raised by single mothers--but ACO is vacuous.

Women are embarrassing in their phony virtue signaling and tyranny. They take over: Jezebel spirit unleashed.

When that tyrannical bad mother Jezebel takes over, watch out! They are meaner than men, caveat!

FEMALE POWER DRIVE

From being their victim I learned how to lead em. I will never lead like that: the female dumb downs.

Through your silence they hear the sirens but when you were trying to explain they only shut down.

I mimicked my feminist dominant mother for years--not even knowing--but now have tenderness/glowing.

If you're caught in a scapegoat system you must walk away. Let your life open up/let them be stopped.

The system compels all roles which are interlocking. Knowing this is relieving esp after triangulation.

To become renowned is to have *overcome* the family from which you sprung-- that's just us humans.

RX: PRUNE YOUR LIFE FOR SUCCESS

I pruned my life for success by unsubbing from 200 political channels--I'm done with this world so dull.

I pruned my life of stuff, people, past-times and food so bring it on Lord, I'm ready to come unglued.

Stop past-remorsing--you allowed disaster because you lost your will to resist due to mental illness.

It was just a lower level: those days you didn't know any better, when you felt compelled to let in danger.

No doubt you feel shaken, it's scary what happened. It wasn't fair but God was there and you'll be doublin'.

To understand the dem's absurd behavior you gotta understand: all these years they felt superior and glad!

You learned lessons from having face pushed in the mud. They didn't--they even think dems are good.

FEMALE POWER DRIVE

There's always strings attached and the most invisible become visible when God condemns the rats.

WHAT HAPPENED TO US

By default we all went liberal and it was horrible.

Instead of remorsing over the past see it as a lower level. All events are explained: culprits/victims.

You were weak back then and brought it on: they're compulsion to sin cuz they were lower companions.

The utter unfairness of the past gave you fire. You need that underbelly for new life of expression of ire.

Lower level: The wicked men are in a silly woman's house who was so weak she let in the creeps.

Your trials gave you that necessary fire to achieve your genius lofty goals which are way out there.

What I learned: If you don't get strong they'll run you right over. Pearls before swine: trampled by clutter.

It was from all your evil associations--the people you brought to my house, bud. You're dangerous, crud.

Don't tell me they're nice--I'll decide that. That's not the point anyway, they're unvetted/some are dirty rats.

PERSONAL REACTIONS

That piece in my puzzle didn't make sense until far later when everything came together: a new life immense.

Jesus came not to unite but to divide. Stop your phony virtue signaling women, being stupid and snide.

We were meant to be together as long as you keep your head above water--no more eye candy brother.

FEMALE POWER DRIVE

Decades in desert wilderness to sort it out: bad fate. Overcame it all: a nice house/tall fence/locked gate.

High wall: each day is my own. All who enter are vetted/on probation forever-- mark of true leader I wager.

Left-handed complement: insult in a velvet glove. Cruelty is in the mixed signals called "love".

Enemies may turn on the fire but God controls the thermostat--for growing from it is where it's at.

The hotter the fire the more amazing your future. God is getting you prepared for destiny I'll betcha.

If God allowed it He knows how to bring good out of it. Repeat: Lord I trust you no matter the bad trip.

There's a lesson in the pain and that's why we face it so don't get hardheaded and move on instead.

The wealthy into status symbols means the left-brain--unable to appreciate the day. What irony, just saying.

If I covet what others have I can't enjoy what I have. Tho' it seems like less it's way more and I'm glad.

BLABBERS, BACKSTABBERS AND ENABLERS

I pity women who blab all day on horn but don't know enough to object to porn, Satan's way into the home.

Only after repentance could I see a beautiful world through the right brain-- lived in a dark box before then.

Insofar as affluence makes unnecessary repentance, they've had it--affording more sin to deal with it.

Addictive process of darkness applies to rich and poor alike--bum may not like it but if pure sees bright.

FEMALE POWER DRIVE

Every sad experience changed me for good. It made me stronger--protected from feminists and hoods.

The pearl within can only be developed in tough times--but they're just one piece in this life of mine.

So she doesn't understand you, forget it. She isn't as smart as you so grow up and don't expect it.

The closer you get the more chance that person is gone forever. I hate that but soon this life is over.

Gotta know how to hold em, how to fold em & when to walk away when the dealin's done. Kenny Rogers

Whether the wife is 30, 35, 40 or whatever she's competing with teen age porn stars--it's the end of her.

Go easy, it's not a contest or competition--it's been laid out for you now just gradually do it to accrue.

DON'T REPRODUCE PAST: HORMONE BLAST

Don't run the bad event through your head even one more time--chemicals flow as if your still in the slime.

Eliminating social obligations is like clearing a cobweb off a mirror: what we want is freedom to soar.

Everything in the past deposited something in the inside. You're not defined by past, you're prepared by it.

It's a SYSTEM: They brought it on--you're lunacy, hon'. Then your shame took over without you knowin'.

For every setback God has already arranged a comeback. Isn't God great? The divine Cure for sad sacks.

For every failure there is restoration. Repentance wipes the slate clean and we're whole again.

FEMALE POWER DRIVE

I use all my energies on this one thing: forgetting what lies behind and reaching on what lies ahead. Paul

There's beauty for ashes, joy for mourning, dancing for heaviness--IF you move forward from the past.

He's gotten older now. He's more like a grandfather than an old buzzard.

Left-handed complement: insult in a velvet glove. Like: "You look so good *for your age.*"

They prefer self-destructive attacks (can't see it) over being reasonable and decent (never count of it).

Difference between happy/positive and the losers/negative is the happy drops the past/is done with it.

It was not fair but God saw what happened and He's a God of Justice and resolution is His promise.

LET GOD BE YOUR VINDICATOR

God I trust You to be my Vindicator, to open the right doors and get me where I'm supposed to be.

Life is too short to carry around old baggage--you're destiny too important, your time too valuable a loss.

Something better is coming. Joy is coming, favor is coming, the fullness of your destiny IF you be forgiving.

To overcome the herd is to cut the curse and if you can let the past go you'll be successful with perks.

When they pull the race card you be sure to pull the Trump card--so we can win, win, win! Diamond and Silk

Why the hell would the democrats do the bidding of the dreamer movement? What about our visions?

FEMALE POWER DRIVE

I have been called "white" for stating the facts. I am not white just right. Michelle Malkin at CPAC

Right has been de-facebooked, detwittered, de-paypalled, deplatformed--deprived of right to a living.

Evil loves evil. They LOVED evil dictator Obama, they HATE giant patriot Trump. Law of Affinity that's all.

San Francisco, a shit-hole, is the epicenter of radical leftism in America and it's getting worse I swear to ya.

The Housewives are caddy women with no values or jobs. They marry into money, social climb or rob.

Liberals look "up" to The Housewives and they look DOWN on middle America and it's values, no jive.

America must give up it's brazen fashions whether we like it or not. International style is modest tho' hot.

REST BEFORE RULE: OLD MOVIES

I'm into old movies: good scripts, great scenes not "effects". The new movies are brazen, loud, chaotic.

You're into sound effects, I'm into neat scripts--go away hicks.

All Time Favorite TV Series: Bonanza and Dallas. These are family friendly alpha males in America.

In those years I persevered but then later, a new house and state living around patriots/good cheer.

I pruned my life of distractions from God and purpose. Like unsubbing from 200 YT channels for instance.

The whole friggin' tragedy gave you necessary AUDACITY. You're done with all conformity to utter tyranny.

FEMALE POWER DRIVE

It's family, faith, freedom and **HARD WORK** which defines middle America--the only reality I swear to ya.

When nice possessions and a glitzy club are all you live for life loses true meaningfulness and more.

FOOD OBSTRUCTIONS (WHILE WAITING)

So fat she can't walk but so trapped by food she needs the crutch and refuses weightloss surgery too.

Like a snake or the drano ad, picture that and that's why I eat once a day and stay thin and quick.

Why is it kids won't eat their vegetables? Cuz they can sense the anti-nutrients (made me disabled).

Fruit's ok, it melts right in like the meat. Fruit and meat: but both camps reject that as a dogma-cheat.

I only sit down to eat once a day when I fill up on fats. Carbs too if I want em, I don't diet and that's that.

If you can't eat/have lost interest in eating why not just have one meal of raw milk and piece cheese?

Raw milk and piece cheese, there's no reason we can live on this with all requirements pleased.

CARNIVORES EAT FRUIT AND LEAVES

Carnivores eat **FRUIT** and **LEAVES** to varying degrees--indulge yourself in these and forget carbs, please!

Food routine: Two raw milkshakes a day plus a snack. Work: Review again and again and then again.

Can't digest anymore--body sees it as an allergen then acid, bubbles, pain, can't sleep. Milkshakes: release!

FEMALE POWER DRIVE

Just can't eat meat, not in my matrix. **LACTO-FRUITARIAN** has been my answer for decades, thanks!

As much raw milk, cream, cheese and butter I care for constrained to 4-8 hr food window then fast (**SOAR**).

Two milkshakes and a snack.

Solid food = pain all day, depression. Liquid diet/lacto & fruit: happy and creative all day, soaring.

Veggies have anti-nutrients, meat makes me sick. What's left? Fruit and dairy as the entire food list.

Tho' you don't like meat you still need animal **FAT** and protein. I'm lovin' humane dairy, so keen!

Look at the beautiful women and handsome men from dairy-centered countries, see what I mean man?

Cats are carnivores dammit--stop feeding them the vegan diet.

Solid food: burp, bubbles, acid, bloat, breathless, takes forever. Milkshakes: energy, beauty/so clever.

Thank God I married a man who doesn't drink or smoke. My guy's overcome those crutches and yokes.

The thinnest cowboy I ever saw said: "When I eat it's the most calorically dense cuz then I must fast".

We're able to change our genetic makeup thru the food we eat and the thoughts and company we keep.

Because I was weak from malnutrition they were able to take me over to near-destruction--yet Salvation.

INDEX: NARCISSISM GOOD AND BAD:

These first five characteristics are actually **GOOD** for a child of God

FEMALE POWER DRIVE

1. A grandiose sense of self-importance
(cuz our God is Great!)

2. A preoccupation with fantasies of unlimited success, power, brilliance, beauty, or ideal love

(cuz our God can do anything!)

3. A belief that he or she is special and unique and can only be understood by other special people

(yes, cuz uniqueness and individuality is Americana, Christian and conservative, vs liberal collectivism which is conformity and misery and we know they don't understand us!)

4. A need for excessive admiration

(it's good to have a good rep in your community, and if we're a child of God it's nice to be admired rather than persecuted and hated!)

5. A sense of entitlement

(Well we ARE entitled to everything that our Father owns and He has plans to prosper us in His promises!)

These are the negative characteristics that will get you labeled "narcissist":

Change these to humility and likability and you can have the first five above which are actually greatness:

STOP THESE TO BE A HAPPY NARCISSIST:

6. Interpersonally exploitive behavior

7. A lack of empathy

8. Envy of others or a belief that others are envious

9. Arrogant and haughty behaviors or attitudes

134 Books: MANUAL FOR SUPERIOR MEN

FEMALE POWER DRIVE

I got to the point where I just wanted to be read no matter the money then it all broke open as God fed.

134 books are done it doesn't matter what they say. I don't have to defend em either, will retire all my days.

They are now available, a helluva seed. It's a huge part of the puzzle of success but I'll wait with joy unceased.

AS SOON AS the Creative Act's complete it attracts pollination to be produced on earth: nature's structure.

Now the Great Work is finally complete I'll go into decline but I'll retire into riches because I did it.

The sense of monumental achievement of an (as-yet unrecognized) world masterpiece is pure bliss.

REST BEFORE RULE: HOW TO BE WHILE WAITING

Knowing there's ONE link and ONE selected time should bring you great relief. Work, wait--float like a leaf.

Just do your work and wait as the cycle completes itself. There's other variables you know, so relax.

You're gonna have to wait for that ONE link--wait to be discovered--because the herd can't be bothered.

You're just gonna have to wait for that ONE moment splitting the miserable past from the bountiful future.

God's timing may not seem just but it is exact. Albert Einstein

God has it all planned: the link to success and the exact moment. Knowing that you can just relax!

It's about who you are while waiting--do you give up easily?

While you wait, prune things down/de-fat. There's always stuff to get rid of maybe God's waiting for that.

FEMALE POWER DRIVE

How you act while waiting is the whole thing. You planned success just by finishing? You must wait sweetie.

While waiting I'm watching 15 seasons of Dallas--anything but wring my hands in fear/anxiousness.

I will **WAIT** on the Lord because I understand: He promised He would bless the work of my hands.

Why worry? You know it's inspired, that God's been with you the whole time so of course He'll have the guy.

Retire into old movies, cooking--anything but what you just completed. Wait on the Lord: the Undefeated.

Unsubbed from political videos and felt better. Creeped back into it and got immediate headache, bitter.

Chew on this: In God's scheme there's only **ONE** right link! And everyone else will pass or say it stinks.

Clear clutter off the table, wipe cobwebs off a mirror: prune of all that's unnecessary, inferior or weird.

PAST HUMILIATIONS GAVE YOU FIRE

Past humiliations give you fire--*charisma*--after having your face pushed in the mud like now in America.

Apart from Me you can do nothing. John 3

You're ignored because you're protected under God's wings until your time has come--and that's soon, hon'

Turn it all off--it's inferior. Now go deep inside and think whatever comes up-- write about it/never stop.

Instead of frantically trying to make it work just realize God has The Plan and you can only interfere.

FEMALE POWER DRIVE

It thrills me to know God will take care of it. He wants me outa the way, to take leisure while I wait for it.

Have a party while you waiteth my Father sayeth.

Stop worrying about remuneration for your work--God's got it covered! It's faith in that first--then discover.

RANDOM THOUGHTS

America is the Prize to Collapse. It's all about overtaking and replacing her, an impossible task.

Elites pour money into feminism to degrade men. They don't want anyone successful but them.

Is it a democracy which is failing or an authoritarian system in the process of succeeding?

Appeasement provokes but strength deters. Unlike now we were safe thru the Trump years.

If an email is insufficient to lay plans and set a date then you know they just wanna bloviate--no way.

Is it good music or screeches from hell? They say "who can tell" but your mom feels she's in hell.

Have highs and lows, ebbs and flows not all loud until it becomes mush: get finesse and variety sis.

He literally erases the past. Now legalistic scholars won't tell you that, neither the Calvinists.

Why do you think He couldn't erase the past? Einstein even showed there is no time, alas.

Feeling music on such deep emotional levels, I'm floating on emotions as deep as the ocean.

100 KAREN KELLOCK BOOKS

AFFINITY OR MISERY
AGELESS CORNUCOPIA
AMERICA AWAKE!
AMERICA'S DAFT ERA
ARTS OF PALEO FASTING
AUTOPHAGY ON CHEATERS
BACKSTABBING NEUROTICS
BETRAYAL TRAUMA
BOOMERS AND BROKENNESS
BOOT ON NECK
CHAMPION GUIDES
COMMIE NUTHOUSE
COMMIES
COMMUNIST SPIRIT
CONTAGION OF MADNESS
CONTAGIOUS MADNESS
CULTURE CLASH BASHED
DAFT LEFT
DAILY FASTARIAN
DAM RATS
DIVERSITY IS CRUELTY
E-RACE WHITE
EVIL FREAKS (Beyond Gross)
THE END OR A BEND?
FEMALE BULLIES AND FEMI-NAZIS
FEMALE CARNALITY
FEMALE DUMB DOWN
FEMALE POWER DRIVE
FEMINISM AND RUIN 1 & 2
FIX FOR MISFITS
FOOLS & TRAMPS
FREEDOM SPEAKING
FRENEMY ENABLER
FRENEMY LIAR
FRENEMY THIEF
FRENEMY TRAITOR
TRENEMY TYRANT
GENIUS IS HELD DOWN
GLOBALISLAM
GOD USES THE FLAWED
HAZE OF THE LATTER DAYS

AUTHOR BIO

Karen Kellock Ph.D.

Ph.D Political Psychology, UCI 1976
Post-Doctoral: UCI Medical School
Department of Psychiatry
Grants NIMH, NIAAA

Ph.D. dissertation "A Systems-Theoretic View of Pathologic Interaction" made an early mark as the "Wife of the Alcoholic Syndrome". Postdoctoral research at UCI Medical, Dept. of Psychiatry on the systems surrounding pathology on NIMH and NIAAA federal grants: _The Contagion of Madness: The Psychology of Neurotic Interaction and Pathological Systems._ Therapy tool Therapeutic Playwriting introduced the play _Mary and Murv: Gruesome Twosomes in the Alcoholic Marriage._ She taught Abnormal Psychology and Pathological Systems Theory at UC and CSU campuses and developed "the Debris Theory of Disease" in five books and website: (www.karenkellock.org): _Champion Guides, Daily Fastarian, Just Skip Dinner, Arts of Paleo Fasting, Ageless Cornucopia. Manual for Superior Men is a_ pick-it-up-anywhere book that you can't put down (20,000 Kellockialisms) and ever on your desktop it should be found (or this Ebook for superior wordsearch of new jargon).

www.ingramcontent.com/pod-product-compliance
Lightning Source LLC
Chambersburg PA
CBHW050759240726
48654CB00008B/559